CLARK, P.
American War of Independance

c

-6 JUN 1995

2 5 NOV 1997

2 · 11 · 88

# AMERICAN WAR OF INDEPENDENCE

A Cherrytree Book

Designed and produced by
A S Publishing

First published 1988
by Cherrytree Press Ltd
a subsidiary of
The Chivers Company Ltd
Windsor Bridge Road
Bath, Avon BA2 3AX

Copyright © Cherrytree Press Ltd 1988

*British Library Cataloguing in Publication Data*
Clark, Philip
    American War of Independence. — (Wars
    that changed the world).
    I. United States—History—Revolution,
    1775-1783
    I. Title    II. Keay, Jack    III. Series
    973.3    E208

    ISBN 0-7451-5005-5

Printed in Italy by New Interlitho, Milan

WARS THAT CHANGED THE WORLD

# AMERICAN WAR OF INDEPENDENCE

*By* Philip Clark
*Illustrated by* Jack Keay *and* Richard Hook

CHERRYTREE BOOKS

# The Thirteen Colonies

Over two hundred years ago, in the mid 1700s, three great European powers – France, Spain and Britain – were engaged in a struggle for control of the vast North American continent.

Britain's possessions at that time consisted of a row of colonies along the Atlantic coast, eventually to become the first thirteen states of the USA. The first attempt to found a British colony, by Sir Walter Raleigh in 1584, had been a failure. A second attempt in 1607 succeeded, however. During the next fifty years, further colonies were established along the east coast, and all eventually came under British control.

Each of the thirteen colonies had its own local government. Most of the colonists were farmers. In the South, the main crops included tobacco, cotton and rice, which were traded with England for manufactured goods.

Virginia tobacco being loaded on to a waiting ship by slave labour. In the South particularly, American colonists imported many of their manufactured goods from Britain. They paid for these by exporting tobacco and other crops. But British merchants pocketed much of the profits, and British laws restricted the colonies' overseas trade.

British
French
Spanish

The 13 Colonies in 1756

Quebec

Canada

Montreal

Lake
Champlain

1

Ticonderoga

Saratoga

Boston

2

NEW YORK

Hudson R.

3    4

New York

5

PENNSYLVANIA

Philadelphia

7

Northwest
Territory

Potomac R.

6

Ohio R.

VIRGINIA

Yorktown

N. CAROLINA

S. CAROLINA

1  NEW HAMPSHIRE
2  MASSACHUSETTS
3  CONNECTICUT
4  RHODE ISLAND
5  NEW JERSEY
6  DELAWARE
7  MARYLAND

GEORGIA

Charleston

Savannah

Pensacola

miles
0        100        200
0    100   200   300
kilometres

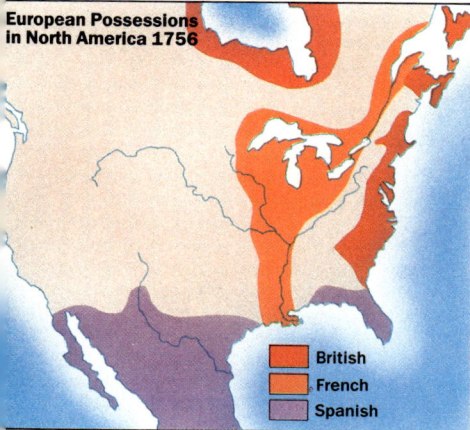

The map, above, shows the
European empires in North
America at the outbreak of
the Seven Years' War in
1756. The power struggle
between Britain, France and
Spain extended across the
Atlantic to the Americas.

The map, right, shows the
thirteen colonies which
eventually became the first
thirteen states of the USA.
Ten were English. New
York was founded by the
Dutch as New Amsterdam.
New Jersey was also
originally Dutch, while
Delaware was settled by the
Swedes. All thirteen
colonies came under British
control.

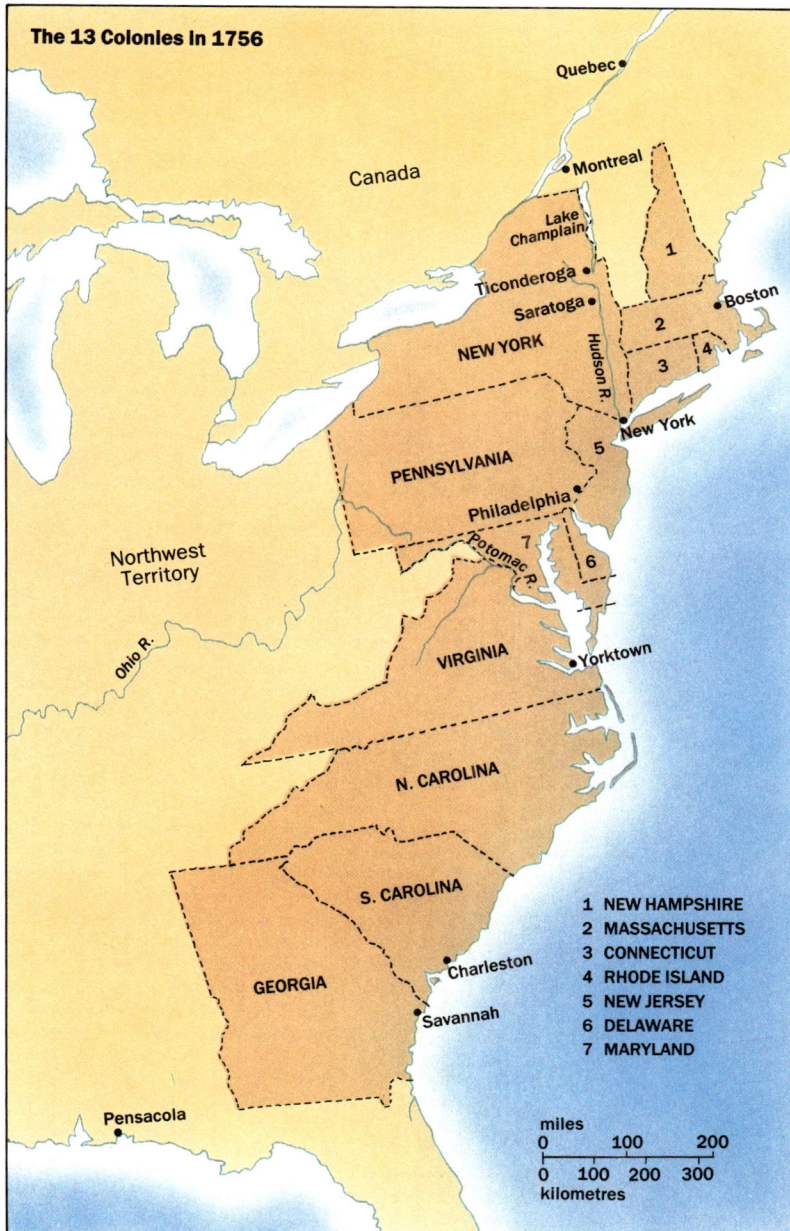

5

# The French and Indian War

French possessions in North America ran from Canada through the Great Lakes, and down the Mississippi to the Gulf of Mexico. To the English-speaking settlers this French empire represented a barrier to their dream of westward expansion. They had turned envious eyes on the lucrative fur trade between the French and the Indian tribes. They also saw great potential riches in the vast territories that lay to the west, since wealth in the colonies was reckoned largely in land.

**The Seven Years' War**
The Seven Years' War was a European conflict that lasted from 1756 to 1763. It was fought between Prussia, supported by Britain, and a group of countries that included France. Fighting between French and English-speaking settlers in North America was similarly almost inevitable. Indeed, the war actually broke out there two years earlier than in Europe. It is known as the French and Indian War, as the French had formed alliances with Indian tribes.

**The Outcome**
George Washington, then a young officer in the Virginia militia (volunteer reserve army), was involved in the fighting. He helped to organize the retreat when a British army under Major General Braddock was ambushed in 1755 by a combined force of French and Indians.

The French hold on Canada was broken in 1759 when a British army under Major General James Wolfe captured Quebec. When the peace treaty was signed in 1763, France lost almost all her North American possessions.

The Boston Massacre, right, took place on 5 March 1770. A group of boys began hurling missiles at the British sentry outside the Custom House. A mob gathered, and the soldiers who hurried up in support of their comrade opened fire, against the orders of their officer. Three men were killed and eight wounded, of whom two later died. Samuel Adams made skilful (if inaccurate) use of the incident in his anti-British propaganda.

### 'No Taxation Without Representation'

The end of the French and Indian War saw an improvement in both the security and prosperity of the thirteen colonies. They no longer had to fear a French invasion from Canada, and some of their merchants had done well from the sale of supplies to the British Army.

Britain, on the other hand, was suffering from debt as a result of the war. The British government felt it reasonable that the colonists should contribute to the cost of the army that had given them security.

The first attempt to raise money was the Stamp Act of 1765, which taxed various official and legal documents as well as newspapers. This tax primarily affected the merchant classes. Some of them, notably Samuel Adams, whipped up popular opposition to the Act. One slogan was 'No taxation without representation'. The colonists objected to being taxed without being represented in the British Parliament.

Britain's King George III, above, attempted to preserve his empire, but Americans saw him as an obstinate tyrant.

# The Boston Tea Party

The British government abolished the Stamp Act in 1766, but still asserted its right to tax the American colonies. For a while it imposed taxes on everyday items such as paper, lead, glass and tea. Then even these taxes were repealed, with the exception of that on tea. The British East India Company was given a monopoly to sell tea to the colonies. This enabled the company to sell its produce at a lower price than tea smuggled from Holland. Some of the colonial leaders became concerned that Americans would turn from the smuggled article to the cheaper (but taxed) English tea.

On 16 December 1773, a band of patriots, thinly disguised as Mohawk Indians, boarded three of the East India Company's ships, and dumped 342 chests of tea into Boston Harbour.

### The 'Intolerable Acts'

King George III reacted angrily when he heard of the 'tea party', and called on Parliament to pass a series of restrictive measures, called the 'Intolerable Acts' by the Americans. Later, Lieutenant General Thomas Gage was appointed governor of Massachusetts, effectively putting the colony under military rule.

### The First Continental Congress

The colonies' reply to these developments was to convene a meeting which came to be known as the First Continental Congress. Delegates met in Philadelphia, the capital of Pennsylvania, in September 1774. They demanded the repeal of the Intolerable Acts as well as a greater say in running their own affairs.

To the Americans, tea was an emblem of British oppression. The Boston Tea Party was a gesture of defiance. Patriots disguised as Indians boarded British ships in Boston Harbour and dumped their cargo of tea. Afterwards the outraged British passed a bill to close the port until the tea – and the tax on it – was paid for.

# Lexington and Concord

The Congress had recommended that the colonies should arm themselves in case of attack. One result of this proposal was the creation of militia forces made up of volunteers called minutemen (they were supposed to be available at one minute's notice).

Meanwhile, the British had obtained information that military stores were being hoarded at the villages of Lexington and Concord, Massachusetts. General Gage sent a detachment of troops to seize the supplies. Messengers set out on horseback to carry the warning that the British were on the march – Paul Revere is the one that history remembers. He was in fact captured before he reached Concord, but the warning got through.

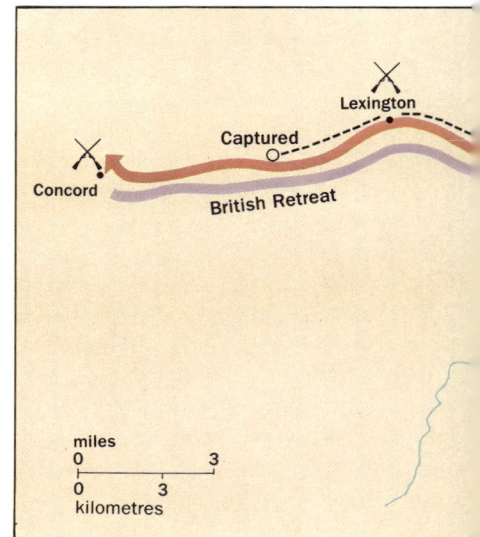

Lexington

Captured

Concord

British Retreat

miles
0          3
0      3
kilometres

The British retreat to Boston under heavy fire, left. The original detachment of about 700 soldiers was reinforced on the return march, bringing total numbers up to 2000 men. Fortunately for the British, most of the rebel fire at this stage of the war was wildly inaccurate. Even so, 73 redcoats were killed against 49 of the patriots.

The map, below, shows Boston and its surroundings in the early stages of the war.

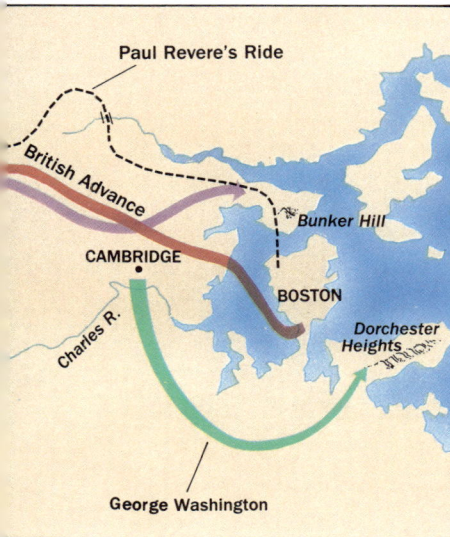

## The Fighting Begins

On 19 April 1775 the British encountered a force of minutemen at Lexington. There was an exchange of fire and several colonists were killed or wounded. No one knows who fired the first shot.

By the time the British reached Concord most of the guns and ammunition had been removed. On their nightmare return march to Boston, the redcoats suffered almost 300 casualties as more and more colonists left their work to take up arms.

Unlike the British, the colonists were at this time very much amateur soldiers. Few had seen any active service. After any fighting, they tended to melt away and return to their farms and villages. Many proved reluctant to leave their own colony if the chances of war took them elsewhere. Later on, recruits signed on for fixed periods of time, and were granted bonuses of land and money for long service.

## The Second Continental Congress

The Second Continental Congress took place in Philadelphia in May 1775. The colonists needed to decide on their next moves. In the meantime, colonial forces had surrounded the British position at Boston.

While the Congress was still in session, news came that a combined force under Benedict Arnold from Massachusetts and Ethan Allen from Vermont had captured crumbling Fort Ticonderoga on Lake Champlain. Among the weapons taken were no less than eighty cannon as well as powder and shot. This was a tremendous windfall for the colonists. Washington wrote later that the need for field guns was 'so great that no Trouble or Expence must be spared to obtain them'.

# A Gentleman from Virginia

The Second Continental Congress agreed to form an 'American Continental Army'. The delegates realized that it was vital for the colonies to act together if they were to have any hope of defeating the British. Then came the question of electing a commander in chief. John Adams, who led the Massachusetts delegation, proposed 'a gentleman from Virginia' – George Washington. Washington was unanimously elected, and further impressed the Congress by his modest speech of acceptance.

**Commander in Chief**
Washington was now aged forty-three, and a substantial land-owner. He volunteered to serve without pay, and to charge for his expenses only. A tall, impressive figure and a splendid horseman, his military experience made him an obvious candidate.

Washington was privately anxious about his new responsibilities. 'I am now Imbarked on a wide Ocean, boundless in its prospect,' he wrote to his brother Jack, 'and from whence, perhaps no safe harbour is to be found.'

**The Battle for Breed's Hill**
During the previous month, the colonial forces had occupied the high ground overlooking Boston. The British, who had been considering a similar move, decided on a frontal attack to dislodge the colonists.

After a series of costly assaults, the British regular troops finally drove the colonists from their positions on Breed's Hill. (The battle is usually named after nearby Bunker Hill.) However, the British losses of 1054 killed

George Washington wore his uniform as a colonel in the Virginia militia throughout the Second Continental Congress, perhaps as a hint that he was available for the chief command. John Adams believed that putting a Southerner in command of a largely New England army would show the world that the colonists were capable of uniting against a common enemy.

Examples of American uniforms and weapons. In the early days of the war, most colonial troops wore civilian clothes. Congress stipulated that, where possible, uniforms should be brown. However, the individual colonies had their own distinctive uniforms. In 1778, a shipment of brown and blue uniform coats arrived from France.

and wounded were much greater than the colonists'. Since the British could only obtain reinforcements by sea across the Atlantic, they could not afford to continue losing men on this scale.

The British claimed a victory, but when news of the casualties reached London, one critic commented that if there were eight more such 'victories' there would be no one left to report them.

General Gage was removed from his command, and was replaced by Lieutenant General William Howe. Howe had previously distinguished himself at the Battle of Quebec as a young colonel in Wolfe's army.

Tomahawk

Officer, Colonel Sargent's Massachusetts Battalion

Sword

Colonial Militiaman

Pistol

Paper cartridge

Ball

Bayonet

French musket

Powder horn

13

# The Siege of Boston

In July 1775, General George Washington took over command of the troops surrounding Boston. The army was short of everything – food, tents, muskets, powder and shot. The men had little idea of military discipline, and one of Washington's chief problems was simply to stop them giving up and going home. He spent much of the rest of the year training and reorganizing his army.

## The Guns of Ticonderoga

In the meantime, Washington had given the task of collecting the cannon from Fort Ticonderoga to an overweight but energetic former bookseller named Henry Knox. Knox organized the huge task of dragging 59 of the guns on ox-drawn sledges over the winter snow to Boston.

Early in 1776, colonial troops occupied the high ground at Dorchester, south of the city. When Knox's artillery arrived, Washington was able to use it to threaten not only the city but the movements of the British fleet, on which Howe's communications depended.

## The British Pull Out

Howe realized that he had lost the initiative, and decided on withdrawal. The entire British Army, plus a number of colonists who had remained loyal to Britain – some ten thousand individuals in all – boarded their ships and set sail for Halifax, Nova Scotia.

Not without a note of pride, Washington was able to announce to Congress: 'It is with the greatest pleasure I inform you that on Sunday last the 17th instant, about 9 o'clock in the forenoon the Ministerial Army evacuated the Town of Boston.'

Private,
40th Regiment

Officer,
Light Infantry

British uniforms were ill suited to the extremes of the American climate. It might take a soldier three hours to get his uniform into parade-ground condition. Officers purchased their commissions, while the rank and file were largely recruited from the slums and jails.

**Private, Jaeger Company**

Brunswick Dragoon's sword

Jaeger Busche rifle

Unable to supply sufficient British troops, George III paid 'head money' to German princelings for mercenaries. Americans referred to the German soldiers as 'Hessians', and newspapers were full of stories of Hessian atrocities. Nearly 30,000 German troops were sent to America.

## The New York Campaign

Washington guessed that the British Army's next move would be an attack on New York which, in his own words, secured 'the free and only communication between the Northern and Southern colonies, which will be entirely cut off by their possessing it, and give them the command of Hudson's River and an easy pass into Canada.'

Washington's intuition proved correct. The British began to arrive in New York in June 1776. The regular army was supported by German mercenaries, always referred to by the colonists as 'Hessians' (many of them came from the German principality of Hesse-Cassel). In all, the British force consisted of over thirty thousand men. It was supported by a large fleet under Vice Admiral Lord Howe (General Howe's brother).

## The Canadian Campaign

Well aware of a possible British attack from Canada, Congress sent an army under Generals Schuyler and Montgomery to secure the Canadian frontier. Washington also sent a force under Benedict Arnold.

Schuyler became ill, but Montgomery and Arnold joined forces near Quebec in December 1775. They attacked the city at night during a snowstorm. The attack failed. Montgomery was killed and Arnold wounded.

Arnold refused to give up, and laid siege to Quebec. The following year, Congress sent reinforcements but the Americans were still forced to retreat by a large British army under Lieutenant General John Burgoyne which sailed up the St Lawrence in the spring of 1776.

The American invasion of Canada had been a spectacular failure, but at least it had made the British divide their forces.

# Declaration of Independence

At the beginning of 1776, many colonists still wished to avoid final separation from Britain. Then, an anonymous pamphlet was published entitled *Common Sense*. The author, who turned out to be an English immigrant called Thomas Paine, argued powerfully for independence. Paine's pamphlet was a significant factor in the decision to cut the ties with the British Crown.

## The Drafting Committee

In June the Congress appointed a committee to draft a document declaring independence from Britain. The committee included John Adams, Benjamin Franklin and Thomas Jefferson. Jefferson was the principal author.

The Declaration stated that the 'United States of America' were 'free and independent'. Jefferson's draft was debated clause by clause, but finally accepted with relatively few changes. The day it was published, 4 July, is celebrated as a public holiday in the USA.

Washington received the news in New York a few days later, and ordered the Declaration to be read to his troops. There could be no going back now: the war would have to be fought to a finish. Either the British would have to subdue the colonists by force, or the colonists would have to hold out until the British were unable – or unwilling – to continue the struggle.

When the Declaration was heard in New York, 'Sons of Liberty' attached ropes to an equestrian statue of King George III, and pulled horse and rider to the ground. Most of the lead was melted down to make bullets – over 40,000 of them. (The king's head was retrieved by loyalists and eventually returned to England.)

The United States flag, above, was designed by Francis Hopkinson in 1777. The present-day version still has thirteen stripes, representing the original thirteen states.

The Congress appointed a committee, left, to draft the Declaration of Independence. Its members were (left to right) Thomas Jefferson, Benjamin Franklin, Roger Sherman, John Adams and Robert Livingston. The Declaration was published on 4 July 1776, still celebrated as a public holiday in the USA.

17

# 'The Game is Pretty Near Up'

While Congress was voting through the Declaration, General Howe appeared off New York and landed troops on Staten Island. The areas surrounding New York City itself were at that time thinly populated, so troops could move freely through the open country.

## The Battle of Long Island

Washington believed that the British attack would be made against Manhattan, but he sent 8000 troops to defend Long Island, which was where the attack in fact came. British and German troops attacked the American positions from both wings and from the rear. Some 2000 colonists were killed, injured or captured.

The colonial troops that survived retreated to fortifications on Brooklyn Heights. There Washington ordered all available small boats to be collected. On the night of 29 August, under cover of darkness and fog, almost 10,000 men were ferried across the East River.

The Battle of Long Island was undoubtedly a British victory, but the final episode was to set a pattern for the future. Washington redeemed his military failure by his masterful handling of the evacuation. Howe won on the field, but failed to follow up his success.

## Retreat to White Plains

Washington decided that he had no alternative but to abandon New York. His confidence in his troops had been shaken, and to add to his difficulties, many of them had signed on only until the end of the year. He retreated up the Hudson River to White Plains. Two forts – Washington and Lee – had been constructed on

The map shows the Hudson River which the colonists lost control of. Fort Washington fell on 16 November 1776 with the loss of nearly 3000 troops and their equipment, as well as large numbers of cannon. Four days later, Fort Lee was captured by Lord Cornwallis. On this occasion the garrison escaped just in time, leaving their half-eaten breakfasts behind them.

opposite banks of the Hudson in a vain attempt to prevent the British sailing up it. The British occupied New York (which soon afterwards was largely destroyed by fire).

Howe's next move was to force Washington out of his position in the hills surrounding White Plains. Washington should have evacuated the forts, but he left it too late. They were captured; 3000 troops surrendered to the British, and large numbers of cannon and other valuable stores were captured.

Washington was forced to retreat again, this time across the River Delaware to New Jersey. In a letter to his brother he wrote 'I think the game is pretty near up.' It was the lowest point of his fortunes.

Washington recrosses the icy Delaware River (Christmas 1776) before attacking the German garrison at Trenton. His army was ferried across by Colonel John Glover's regiment of Marblehead seamen, who had also been responsible for the successful evacuation of Long Island.

# The Tide Begins to Turn

Despite Washington's private fears, his amateur soldiers were soon to give the European professionals a lesson in war. In the eighteenth century, European armies habitually stopped fighting at the approach of winter, to resume the following spring. This was partly because roads became almost unusable in winter. Howe therefore called a halt to the campaign and retired to New York, having established a chain of military posts between himself and Washington's army.

### 'I am Resolved to Take Trenton'

Washington, faced with the possible loss of more of his already depleted army, decided to act. On Christmas night 1776, his army recrossed the Delaware and surprised the Hessian garrison at Trenton. The attack was successful and a thousand German troops were captured.

### Fox Chase at Princeton

Howe responded by sending Major General Lord Cornwallis to 'bag the fox'. Washington planned to slip round the British forces, but his troops were intercepted outside Princeton. The outcome was uncertain for a while, but at the critical moment Washington rode through a hail of fire between the lines to rally his troops. The British fled, leaving their dead and wounded behind.

Washington took his army to their winter quarters at Morristown. Thanks to his modest but timely victories, recruitment increased and many former soldiers returned to the ranks. His achievements also helped to prevent the British Army in Canada from linking up with Howe's forces in New York.

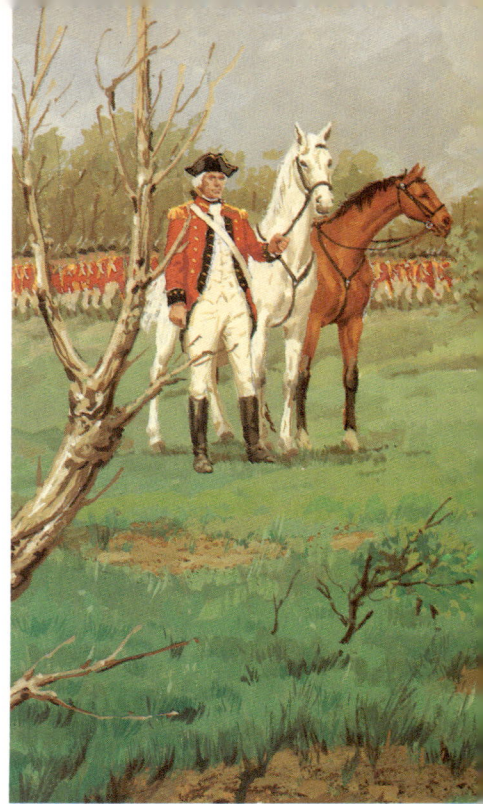

The British General 'Gentleman Johnny' Burgoyne surrenders his sword to General Gates at Saratoga. Gates politely returned it, and invited Burgoyne to dinner in his tent.

Burgoyne's advance down the Hudson had been checked with heavy losses at the two battles of Freeman's Farm (19 September and 7 October 1777).

## Invasion from Canada

An American flotilla under Benedict Arnold had been all but destroyed on Lake Champlain, and the British commander in Canada, Sir Guy Carleton, had proceeded to besiege Fort Ticonderoga. However, he abandoned the siege when he realized that he could expect no reinforcements from General Howe.

In the summer of 1777, a strong British army under Lieutenant General John Burgoyne advanced once more on Fort Ticonderoga, capturing it without a fight. Despite several reverses, Burgoyne pushed on in the hope of linking up with Howe. He was finally trapped at Saratoga, and forced to surrender his force of over 5000 men to Major General Horatio Gates.

General Clinton, who was advancing up the Hudson to reinforce Burgoyne, retreated to New York when he heard news of the surrender.

Gates' victory at Saratoga encouraged France to give official recognition to the United States. The treaty of military support was signed on 6 February 1778.

# The Philadelphia Campaign

Howe's main plan for his 1777 campaign was to capture the American 'capital' of Philadelphia. The rules of war laid down that victory must follow the occupation of the enemy capital. The American nation, however, was still young enough for its government simply to pack its bags and move to a capital elsewhere.

Even so, Washington positioned his army to defend Philadelphia. Outmanoeuvred by Howe at Brandywine Creek, he was forced to retreat, though in reasonably good order. In September, Cornwallis's army marched triumphantly into Philadelphia, while Howe set up his headquarters at Germantown. Washington devised a plan of attack on Germantown that proved too complicated for his troops to carry out, and he suffered a further defeat.

Washington and Lafayette watch as Baron von Steuben drills their troops at Valley Forge. Von Steuben was a Prussian adventurer who claimed (untruthfully) to have been a general in the army of Frederick the Great. He was nevertheless a thoroughly professional soldier who transformed the performance of the Continental Army.

## Valley Forge

Despite other defeats, the American victory at Saratoga convinced several European powers, notably France, that the Americans stood a chance of winning the war. From this point on, the colonists were able to count on active French support, including the powerful French fleet. Many European officers joined the American cause, including the young Marquis de Lafayette.

In December 1777 Washington's choice of winter quarters for his army was an exposed, bleak and hilly site called Valley Forge. This lay between Philadelphia and the Congress, now at York, Pennsylvania. While Howe's officers amused themselves in Philadelphia, a quarter of Washington's troops died of cold, exposure and starvation on the snow-covered hillsides. And yet in the following spring, a tougher, more formidable army emerged from this grim training ground.

## The Battle of Monmouth

Meanwhile Howe had been replaced by General Sir Henry Clinton. Clinton was ordered to abandon Philadelphia and return to New York. This move gave Washington the opportunity to attack him on the march. Washington put Major General Charles Lee in command of his advance guard, and attacked on a blazing June day in 1778 at Monmouth Court House.

Lee bungled the attack, and only Washington's personal intervention prevented disaster. As it was, the well-drilled American troops were able to stave off a British counter-attack, and the battle ended inconclusively. Lee was later dismissed from the army. No one realized it at the time, but the Battle of Monmouth was destined to be the last major engagement of the war in the North.

**Major General Charles Lee**
A former British regular officer, who also claimed to be a general in the Polish army, Lee had been one of the original four major generals appointed to serve under Washington. A conceited and difficult personality, Lee had carelessly allowed himself to be captured by the British in December 1776. He was later released in an exchange of prisoners, but not before he had discussed with his captors a plan for defeating the rebels. After his disastrous handling of the Battle of Monmouth, Lee was dismissed from the army.

# The War in the South

The British had always to some extent pinned their hopes on attracting the support of loyalists – Americans who continued to support the Crown. With deadlock in the North, the British decided to concentrate their efforts on the southern colonies, where they expected more support from the civilian population.

In 1778, Clinton sent a British force to Savannah, which was at that time the capital of Georgia, the southernmost of the thirteen colonies. By early 1779, the British appeared to control the whole state. In September a French fleet under Admiral d'Estaing arrived at the mouth of the Savannah River. A combined assault on the port by d'Estaing and Major General Benjamin Lincoln proved a costly failure, and Lincoln retreated up the coast to Charleston, South Carolina.

## Charleston Surrenders

At the end of 1779, Clinton sailed from New York with 8000 men. British frigates entered Charleston Harbour, and British troops blocked Lincoln's line of retreat inland. On 12 May 1780, Lincoln surrendered. The loss of his army of 5500 men, together with their military supplies, was perhaps the biggest single disaster suffered by the colonists in the entire war.

Clinton returned to New York, leaving Lord Cornwallis in command in Georgia and South Carolina. It now seemed that the two most southerly colonies were firmly back under British rule. Against Washington's advice, the Congress put General Gates of Saratoga fame in charge of a southern army. His instructions were to loosen Cornwallis's grip on the southern states.

**Benedict Arnold's Treachery**
There are few more curious characters in the war than Benedict Arnold. Of undoubted bravery in the field, he distinguished himself in battle on numerous occasions. Then, embittered by the promotion over his head of his juniors, and personally extravagant, he obtained the command of West Point Fort, which he arranged to betray to the British for money. However, Arnold's British messenger, Major John André (who had been a friend of Arnold's wife) was caught while disguised as a civilian. André was hanged as a spy, and Arnold deserted to the British, who made him a brigadier.

Gates advanced on the British port at Camden, South Carolina, but was soundly defeated by a smaller British force in August 1780. He was belatedly replaced by Major General Nathanael Greene, but meanwhile the energetic Cornwallis had sent a force of American loyalists into North Carolina.

The loyalists were overwhelmed at Kings Mountain on 7 October. Meanwhile the main British Army was being harried by small militia units. In March 1781 Greene attacked Cornwallis at Guilford Court House. Cornwallis was victorious after a desperate struggle, but his army was much weakened and he himself was now ill. He led his troops eastward to Wilmington, North Carolina.

## Britain's Indian Allies

Many of the Indian tribes realized that they were threatened by the colonists' westward expansion. The British were therefore able to buy Indian support with weapons and hard cash.

The Six Nations of the Iroquois attacked settlers in New York and Pennsylvania until Washington sent a punitive expedition against them in 1779.

In the South, the Cherokee raided the Carolinas and Georgia under their chief Dragging Canoe. Finally, it was the Spanish who cut off British supplies to the Cherokee by occupying the ports of Pensacola and Mobile in the Gulf of Mexico. The colonists deplored the use of Indian irregulars, because the Indians followed their own rules of warfare, which included killing women and children and torturing prisoners. They believed that the British paid Indians for American scalps. The British agent at Detroit was given the nickname of 'Hair-Buyer'.

# The War at Sea

Because there were so few naval battles, it is easy to overlook the importance of sea power in the war. The contest was about Britain's control over her colonies, and this control could only be maintained by a powerful fleet.

At the outbreak of war, Britain had almost complete naval supremacy. She could land and withdraw armies almost at will at any point on the east coast. As the war progressed, this state of affairs changed. The most important factor was a treaty made in 1778 between the colonies and France.

## The Alliance with France

From this point onwards, command of the American coastal waters passed back and forth between the British and the French. In June 1780, a French squadron appeared at Newport, Rhode Island, with 4000 troops under the command of the Comte de Rochambeau. The French were however blockaded by a superior British fleet under Lord Rodney. When the French fleet was finally able to evade the blockade, it changed the course of the war.

## The American Navy

The colonists did have their own tiny navy, but they could never contemplate meeting a British fleet in a general engagement. Most American successes came from her privateers. These were privately-owned vessels commissioned by the Congress to raid enemy shipping. The privateers captured numerous British merchant ships and made a considerable nuisance of themselves but did not have a significant effect on the outcome of the war.

**John Paul Jones**
John Paul Jones is the best-known captain of the American commerce raiders. His most famous battle took place off the coast of England in September 1779. Jones's flagship, known to history as the *Bonhomme Richard*, fought a gunnery duel with a British frigate, HMS *Serapis*. Jones's ship was badly damaged and started to take in water. Called upon to surrender, he is said to have replied 'I haven't begun to fight yet'. (Historians continue to argue about his exact words.)

Jones grappled the *Serapis* and carried her by boarding, with the support of a French ship called the *Alliance*. Cut free, the *Bonhomme Richard* filled and sank, but Jones sailed the *Serapis* in triumph to France.

**John Paul Jones refused to surrender during his fight with HMS *Serapis*. He was one of several daring American captains who took the war into British waters. Jones had an adventurous life. Born in Scotland, he later served as an admiral in the Russian navy.**

# Yorktown

The year 1781 began disappointingly for the Americans. Cornwallis's victory at Camden had apparently left him in control of the southern states. Washington, meanwhile, was faced with the mutiny of part of his army, as the troops protested against harsh conditions, lack of food, and worthless money printed by Congress. Washington had to use force to restore order.

In the spring Cornwallis decided to move against Virginia (to the dismay of Clinton who was technically his superior), and sent in the renegade Benedict Arnold. Washington retaliated with troops commanded by von Steuben and Lafayette. Expecting reinforcements by sea, Cornwallis moved to Yorktown and began to fortify it.

## Washington Moves South

In August, the French fleet sailed for Chesapeake Bay, Virginia. Washington had been planning a joint attack on New York, but instead he moved his army to Virginia to link up with the French. A British fleet sailed in pursuit of the French, but came off second best in the ensuing fight, with five ships seriously damaged. In the meantime, a second French fleet under the Comte de Grasse had slipped into Chesapeake Bay. The French were now too powerful for the British to attack, so they returned to New York, leaving Cornwallis cut off by land and sea.

Cornwallis was heavily outnumbered. On 9 October the French politely invited Washington to fire the first shot of the siege of Yorktown. Cornwallis's earthworks were steadily shot to pieces, and the British earl decided that his only hope lay in a breakout.

The attempt was a failure, and Cornwallis, reluctant to

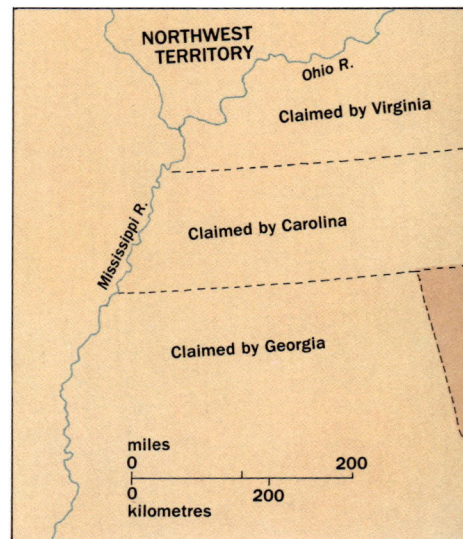

The map, above, shows the southern states, where the outcome of the war was finally decided.

The British surrender at Yorktown, right, effectively ended the war. Cornwallis, who claimed to be ill, sent his deputy, Brigadier General Charles O'Hara, to hand over his sword. Washington refused to deal with a subordinate, and directed O'Hara to surrender to Major General Benjamin Lincoln.

The Southern States

sacrifice his men to no purpose, surrendered. On 19 October 1781 the capitulation documents were signed. Clinton, who had sailed that day from New York with a relieving force, turned back when he heard the news.

It was, however, to be another year before the war finally dragged to its conclusion. On 12 April 1782 the temporary French naval superiority came to an end when de Grasse was beaten by Lord Rodney at the Battle of the Saintes. Lacking naval support, the French Army returned to France later in the year.

Washington's army returned to New York, where Clinton was replaced by Sir Guy Carleton. The British evacuated Charleston and Savannah, and a new government in London opened peace negotiations with the Americans.

# Peace

A preliminary peace treaty was signed in Paris in November 1782 and ratified (approved) by the United States on 19 April the following year. The final treaties, which included those with France and Spain, were not signed until 3 September 1783.

The United States now extended from the Atlantic to the Mississippi in the West, and from Canada (which Britain retained) to the border with Florida. Spain kept Florida and the lands west of the Mississippi. France, which had done so much to help the American cause, had to be content with a few colonies in the West Indies.

So ended the War of Independence. The United States of America grew steadily, by purchase and conquest, to become the richest and most powerful nation on earth.

The last British troops are rowed to their ship in New York Harbour on 25 November 1783. Britain shrugged off its defeat and proceeded to carve out a new empire in India. The Americans elected Washington as the first president of the new nation, and enshrined freedom in its constitution.

# Events of the War

**1773**
| | |
|---|---|
| 10 May | Tea Act |
| 16 Dec | Boston Tea Party |

**1774**
| | |
|---|---|
| 5 Sept | First Continental Congress opens in Philadelphia |

**1775**
| | |
|---|---|
| 19 April | Fighting breaks out at Lexington and Concord |
| 10 May | Second Continental Congress opens Americans capture Fort Ticonderoga |
| 15 June | Washington named Commander in Chief |
| 17 June | Battle of Bunker Hill (Breed's Hill) |
| 30-31 Dec | Americans fail to capture Quebec |

**1776**
| | |
|---|---|
| 17 March | British evacuate Boston |
| 4 July | Declaration of Independence published |
| 27 Aug | Battle of Long Island |
| 15 Sept | British occupy New York |
| 16 Nov | British capture Fort Washington |
| 20 Nov | British capture Fort Lee |
| 26 Nov | Battle of Trenton |

**1777**
| | |
|---|---|
| 3 Jan | Battle of Princeton |
| 6 July | British capture Fort Ticonderoga |
| 11 Sept | Battle of Brandywine |
| 19 Sept | First Battle of Freeman's Farm |
| 26 Sept | British occupy Philadelphia |
| 4 Oct | Battle of Germantown |
| 7 Oct | British beaten at Second Battle of Freeman's Farm |
| 17 Oct | Burgoyne surrenders at Saratoga |
| 19 Dec | Washington moves his army to Valley Forge |

**1778**
| | |
|---|---|
| 6 Feb | Americans sign treaty with France |
| 28 June | Battle of Monmouth |
| 29 Dec | British occupy Savannah, Georgia |

**1779**
| | |
|---|---|
| 21 June | Spain declares war on Britain |
| 23 Sept | British frigate *Serapis* captured by John Paul Jones |

**1780**
| | |
|---|---|
| 12 May | Americans under Benjamin Lincoln surrender at Charleston |
| 16 Aug | Battle of Camden |
| 7 Oct | Battle of Kings Mountain |

**1781**
| | |
|---|---|
| 15 March | Battle of Guilford Court House |
| 15 Sept | French beat off British fleet in Chesapeake Bay |
| 28 Sept | Siege of Yorktown begins |
| 19 Oct | Cornwallis surrenders at Yorktown |

**1782**
| | |
|---|---|
| 12 April | Naval battle of the Saintes restores British command of the sea |
| 11 July | British evacuate Savannah |
| 30 Nov | Preliminary peace treaty signed in Paris |
| 14 Dec | British evacuate Charleston |

**1783**
| | |
|---|---|
| 19 April | United States ratifies preliminary peace treaty |
| 3 Sept | Final peace treaty signed in Paris formally ends the war |
| 25 Nov | Last British troops leave New York |

# Index